AIRPLANES

© 1994 Franklin Watts

Franklin Watts
95 Madison Avenue
New York, NY 10016

Library of Congress Cataloging-in-Publication Data

Richardson, Joy.
    Airplanes / Joy Richardson
        p. cm. – (Picture science)
    Includes index.
    ISBN 0-531-14324-4
    1. Airplanes – Juvenile literature. [1. Airplanes.] I. Title.
    II. Series: Richardson, Joy. Picture science.
    TL547.R48 1994
    629.133'34–dc20   93-42184
                                                        CIP AC

10 9 8 7 6 5 4 3 2 1

Editor: Belinda Weber
Designer: Janet Watson
Picture researcher: Sarah Moule
Illustrators: Robert and Rhoda Burns

Photographs Eye Ubiquitous © Geoff Redmayne 10t, © A Carroll 28;
Quadrant 10b, 12; Robert Harding Picture Library 18, 21,
© Geoff Renner 15; Tony Stone Worldwide title page, 26,
© Hideo Kurihara 16; © Mark Wagner 23; Zefa cover, 7, 9, 24

Printed in Malaysia

AIRPLANES

Joy Richardson

FRANKLIN WATTS

New York • Chicago • London • Toronto • Sydney

Flying through the air

For thousands of years people
looked up into the sky and
dreamed of flying like the birds.
Many people tried but failed.

Two hundred years ago,
people found that hot-air balloons
could lift them into the sky.

Then inventors began to work
on flying machines with wings.

First they made gliders that
floated through the air
like hang gliders today.

Engine power

Gliders cannot travel far
or stay in the air for very long.
Airplanes need power
to make real journeys.

In 1903, the Wright brothers flew
the first airplane with an engine.
The engine drove a propeller
that pushed the plane
forward through the air.

Many early airplanes were biplanes.
They needed double wings for strength.

Pilots steered by moving controls
that pulled on wires attached
to the wings and the tail.

Wings

Wings lift the airplane in the air.

Airplane wings are
shaped like bird wings.
They are round in front
and pointed at the back.
They are curved on top
and flatter underneath.

This shape is called an airfoil.
It makes the air flow smoothly
around the wing and lifts the plane up.

Modern airplane wings are
light but very strong.

Jet engines

At first, airplane engines had
pistons like car engines.
The pistons went up and down,
turning a rod that led to the propeller.

Jet engines are more powerful
and work by sucking in air and
squashing it up to make it hot.
Then fuel catches fire in the
hot air and makes the air expand.

Hot gases rush out like
air from a balloon,
pushing the airplane forward.

This force is called thrust.

cold air

hot gases

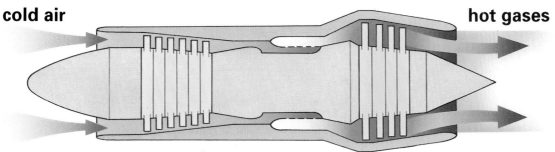

Propeller blades

Piston engines drive propellers
around to make the plane fly.

Some jet engines also use
propellers for extra thrust.

Propeller blades have an
airfoil shape, like wings.

When front propellers turn around
they screw into the air and
pull the airplane forward.

Helicopters have blades on top
that lift the helicopter up
and pull it forward.

Cutting through the air

As the plane speeds forward,
air bumps into it and slows it down.
This force is called drag.

Airplane shapes are designed
to cut down on drag.

Air slips easily around the
pointed nose of the plane,
along the circular body,
and past the tail fin.

The plane is smoothly
plated with metal sheeting and
the wheels can be tucked away.

Inside

The plane's long, round body
is called the fuselage.
It is made of light but sturdy materials.

In a jumbo jet, the top part
contains rows of seats for
hundreds of passengers.

In the bottom part, there is
a huge space for cargo.

Toilets empty into tanks below.
Meals are stored in galleys,
where they are heated and
ready to serve.

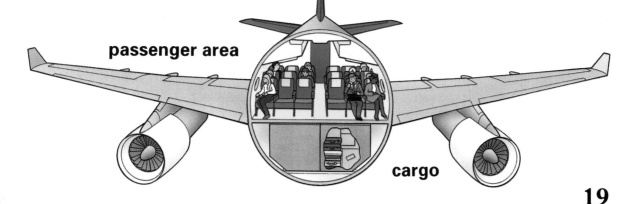

passenger area

cargo

Pilots at work

Pilots control the airplane
from the cockpit in the plane's nose.

Above the clouds, the view from
the window is of little help so pilots
have to rely on their instruments.

They have hundreds of
knobs, switches, and dials
all around them, and computer
screens to display information clearly.

The pilots steer, or they use
the automatic pilot and just check
on the computer as it flies the plane.

Up, down, and around

The pilot uses hand and foot controls
to move the rudder and flaps
on the wings and tail.

Flaps catch the air and
make the plane move up or
down or tilt to one side.

In aerobatic displays,
planes can be made to
roll over or do a loop.

Long flaps on the wings help
to slow the plane down
as it comes in to land.

Jet fighters

Jet fighters can fly very fast and pick up speed very quickly.

They have computers to guide them to their target and radar to track enemy aircraft.

The Harrier jump jet can lift off without a runway, by blasting air downward from its engines.

The Stealth bomber is shaped like a bat to avoid enemy radar.

The Tomcat's wings swing back after take-off, making it more streamlined for faster flying.

Faster than sound

The Concorde is a supersonic airplane,
which means it can travel
faster than sound.

It can cross the Atlantic between
Britain and the United States twice as
fast as other passenger planes.

The Concorde is long and thin
with a pointed nose.
It has swept-back wings to
cut down drag at high speeds.

It is the only supersonic
passenger plane in the world.

Airplane facts

The fastest jet airplane is the Lockheed Blackbird spy plane, which can fly at over 1,860 miles per hour (3,000 km per hour).

The fastest passenger airliner is the Concorde, which cruises at over 1,240 miles per hour (2,000 km per hour).

The Boeing 747 jumbo jet is the biggest passenger airliner. It can take up to 600 passengers.

Index